NOW YOU CAN READ.....
THE SERMON ON THE MOUNT

STORY RETOLD BY LEONARD MATTHEWS

ILLUSTRATED BY CLIVE UPTTON

Published by Rourke Publications, Inc., P.O. Box 3328, Vero Beach, Florida 32964. Copyright © 1984 by Rourke Publications, Inc. All copyrights reserved. No part of this book may be reproduced in any form without written permission from the publisher. Printed in the United States of America.

   The Publishers acknowledge permission from Brimax Books for the use of the name "Now You Can Read" and "Large Type For First Readers" which identify Brimax Now You Can Read series.

Library of Congress Cataloging in Publication Data

Matthews, Leonard.
   The sermon on the mount.

   (Now you can read—Bible stories)
   Summary: Retells stories Jesus told while preaching to the people.
   1. Sermon on the mount—Juvenile literature.
2. Bible stories, English—N.T. Matthew.
[1. Sermon on the mount.   2. Bible stories—N.T.]
I. Title.   II. Series.
BT380.2.M35   1984   232.9'54   84-15124
ISBN 0-86625-307-6

GROLIER ENTERPRISES CORP.

NOW YOU CAN READ. . . .
THE SERMON ON THE MOUNT

Jesus often spoke to the people about God. Speeches about God are known as "sermons." Jesus began to give sermons when He was a boy. He was then working in the carpenter's shop which belonged to Joseph. Joseph was the husband of Mary, who was the mother of Jesus. One day in Jerusalem, Jesus was missing.

Mary found Him
in the Great Temple talking to many
wise men. He was answering their
questions. The wise men were all
amazed. He was so smart.

"Why are you here?" asked Mary.
She was angry.
Quietly Jesus told her that He was
teaching the wise men about His
Father. By "Father" Jesus meant God.
Jesus was the Son of God. When He
grew up, Jesus loved to talk to all
people, rich and poor.

He also loved to talk to children.

Once some mothers brought their children to Jesus so that He might  bless them. The disciples, the followers of Jesus, thought He was too busy to bother with them. They told the mothers to go away. Jesus said "No, let the children come to Me. The Kingdom of God belongs to them." Then, He blessed the children.

Once a rich young man came to speak to Jesus. He owned a big house. He had many men and women to wait on him. Even if he wanted a cup of water, someone would pour it for him.

"I have always lived by God's teaching," he said to Jesus, "but I want to be really good. What should I do?" Jesus knew that he was very rich.

"Sell all you have, give your money to the poor and follow Me," said Jesus.

The young man was very unhappy.
"Money means nothing to God,"
Jesus told him. "It is easier for a
camel to pass through the eye of a
needle than for a rich man to
enter the Kingdom of God."
The young man went home to
think about what he should do.
Another time, Jesus was at a
feast in another rich man's house.

Everybody knew about the rich man's feasts. Today many poor people had rushed to his house. They were all hoping that he would send out some food for them to eat. Jesus knew this. He spoke to the rich man.

"When you give a feast," He said, "do not invite your friends. They will only invite you to their feasts in return."

"Then whom should I invite?" asked the rich man.

"The poor, the sick, the lame and the blind people," replied Jesus. "Of course, they cannot invite you to a feast in return but you will be blessed and remembered for your kindness."

One day Jesus was writing on a sandy
floor with His finger. In those days
people did not have paper and pens,
so sometimes they would scribble in
the sand.

Some priests brought a woman to Him. "She has broken the law," they said. "She must be stoned. That is the proper punishment. Do you agree?" Jesus looked up and replied, "If there is one among you who has never broken the law, he should throw the first stone."

The priests glared. Then, because they had all broken the law at some time, they went away.

"Where are the men who would have punished you?" Jesus asked the woman.

"The priests have gone," the woman replied.

"Then you go, too," Jesus said. "I will not punish you, but be good in the future."

At another time, Jesus was sitting with His disciples. "After I die, I will return," He told them. "You must always be ready for me when I come."

Then Jesus told His disciples the story of the ten bridesmaids. When Jesus lived, it was the job of the bridesmaids to bring the groom to the place where the wedding was to be. At this wedding the groom was late. Five of the ten bridesmaids had fallen asleep. It was night when the groom arrived. In those times, people used to light their homes with oil lamps.

The five bridesmaids who had fallen asleep had not lighted their lamps. They were foolish. Now they could not see in the dark. The five wise bridesmaids had stayed awake. Their lamps were lit.

The five wise bridesmaids were ready to take the groom to the wedding. "Be like the five wise bridesmaids," said Jesus. "Be ready for my return."

On another day, Jesus gave a sermon about a man who, late one night, knocked on the door of a friend's house.

"Someone I know has just arrived," he cried out. "I have no food for him. Please lend me five loaves."

It was only after he had asked many times for the five loaves that his friend came down and handed him the bread. Then Jesus looked at his listeners. "Knock on God's door by praying to Him," He said. "In this way He will hear you and help you."

One day many men and women were waiting to hear Jesus speak. "Please talk to them," a disciple said to Jesus. Jesus was only too happy.

The sermon Jesus gave that day is famous. Because it took place on a hillside, it is called "The Sermon on the Mount."

"Blessed are the poor," Jesus began. "The Kingdom of Heaven is theirs. Blessed are those who are sad. They shall be made happy. God blesses those who are gentle, those who wish to be good and those who are merciful. Those who are pure in heart will understand God's words. Try always to keep the peace. God will then call you His children."

Jesus ended with these words. "Blessed are those who are punished simply for being right and for believing in Me." As He finished speaking, Jesus took the hands of the children around Him. How they loved Him!

All these appear in the pages of the story. Can you find them?

The boy Jesus

wise bridesmaid

wise man

serving maid

priest

Jesus

Now tell the story in your own words.